BOOK DESCRIPTION

Many of us take for granted the fact that we can speak to others with ease. In fact, we forget that we once had to be taught how to properly speak and converse with others. For those comfortable speaking with others, the skill is not questioned. But those who

feel anxious and uncomfortable speaking with others in different social situations will oftentimes simply accept that their nerves and inability to speak will never change.

Of course, this is far from the truth. Speaking with others and being a good conversationalist are skills that can be developed, practiced, and improved, just like any other skill.

This is where this book comes in to help. Within these pages, you will find tips and suggestions in addition to different conversation starters that will help you become an impressive conversationalist, even if you are not one already.

Now, what are you waiting for? Stop being silent, and let's start talking!

BECOME A GREAT CONVERSATIONALIST

CONVERSATION QUESTIONS AND RESPONSES

Godfrey E Butler

© Copyright 2021 Godfrey E Butler

All rights reserved.

Disclaimer Notice:

Please note the information contained within this document is for educational and entertainment purposes only. All effort has been executed to present accurate, up to date, reliable, complete information. No warranties of any kind are declared or implied. Readers acknowledge that the author is not engaged in the rendering of legal, financial, medical or professional advice. The content within this book has been derived from various sources. Please consult a licensed professional before attempting any techniques outlined in this book.

By reading this document, the reader agrees that under no circumstances is the author responsible for any losses, direct or indirect, that are incurred as a result of the use of the information contained within this document, including, but not limited to, errors, omissions, or inaccuracies.

TABLE OF CONTENTS

INTRODUCTION

Being a good conversationalist is a skill that is practiced and developed over time. Whether you are trying to develop a new skill or hone the skill you already have, it is wise to continuously practice and pay attention to how you converse with others.

To help guide you through the development of your conversational skills, this book has been divided into five chapters. The first chapter includes some general suggestions and tips on how to not only become a more confident conversationalist but also how to appear more confident to others until your true confidence shines through.

The following four chapters will include the conversation starters. One common trait shared by those individuals skilled in the art of conversation is that they know which conversation subjects are appropriate for the situation and which are not. For this reason, to help you better understand the art of conversing, the conversation starters have been divided into categories and chapters that focus on different social situations.

Within each chapter, there will be a brief rationale explaining how these conversation starters will be useful to you and possible responses to the conversation starters. You'll see how you can respond if the question is posed to you and possible follow-up questions to ask after your partner answers.

After completing the book, you will have all of the necessary tools to become a skilled conversationalist that others enjoy being around.

Of course, none of that can happen if you do not take the first step. So, let us take the first step together.

CHAPTER 1

GENERAL TIPS FOR CONVERSATIONS

Before looking at the different kinds of conversation starters, you need to understand which character traits are shared between individuals skilled in the art of conversation. Although each successful individual has their own method of conversing with others, seven commonly shared characteristics are associated with making them strong conversationalists (Griffin, 2018). These traits are being prepared, paying attention to body language, not responding with one-word answers, asking open-ended questions, showing genuine interest, listening, and not oversharing.

Come Prepared

The first step to becoming a better conversational partner is to prepare yourself for the conversation. This does not mean you have to memorize hundreds of conversation topics, nor do you have to research and be knowledgeable about every possible response to every possible question. Instead, this means that it is good to know and understand what is expected of you conversation-wise in different social situations.

For instance, in a formal or business situation, it is expected that you present yourself in a more dignified manner than you would when you are hanging out with a group of friends. In business situations such as conferences, you should be able to begin and hold your own conversation with others as it is not guaranteed that others will approach you.

Alternatively, in situations where the environment is much more casual, the expectations will be different. In more casual settings, such as friendly group hangouts, the pressure to continue the conversation with someone else is not as strong as it is in more formal social situations.

Another way of coming prepared is to research who will be attending the event. For example, if you are attending a business convention, what other companies will be there? After all, if it is a conference where only local companies are going to be present, questions about commute or where they are from will not be considered appropriate. If it is a first date or more casual situation, it is important to know who will be attending to better gear the questions accordingly. If it is a first date with someone you met online, you may want to ask questions about their experience with the online dating platform.

Pay Attention to Body Language

Another important aspect for those individuals who want to be better at conversing is to pay attention to the body language of everyone involved. First of all, be aware of your own body language. If you are shrugging, hunched over, or not facing your partners, you will come off as unconfident, uninterested in the conversation, and not present in the situation. This will lead to individuals thinking you are rude, don't belong there, or that you allowed your nerves to take over. Although there is nothing inherently wrong with some of these consequences, they are counterproductive to the goal of being considered a well-rounded conversationalist. Therefore, it is important to stand up straight, face the individuals you are talking to, make eye contact, and speak clearly and slowly. By doing so, you will present yourself as confident, interested, and skilled in the art of conversation.

It is also important to pay attention to the body language of those you are talking to. For instance, if your conversation partners are hunched over, fidgeting, or not making eye contact with you, this could mean that they are uncomfortable or uninterested in your questions. Either way, their body language is telling you that you must shift your method of conversation, the style of your questions, or your body language and physical presentation. The goal of a well-rounded conversationalist is to ensure that their partners are comfortable and remain interested; otherwise, the conversation will be easily forgotten or remembered for the wrong reasons.

Don't Respond 'Yes' or 'No'

A third aspect of being a good conversationalist comes from how you respond to others' questions and comments. Don't simply answer the question with 'yes' or 'no.' Of course, some questions ask for a 'yes' or 'no' response; however, your response should never simply include one of those two words. Instead, take up a practice that is commonly used in improv. Within this acting skill, the rule is to say 'yes and…' In conversations, you can do this by answering either 'yes' or 'no' and adding a qualifying sentence to it, one that can justify or explain your answer.

Allowing yourself to give more than one-word answers, even if the question warrants that, will make you seem genuinely interested in the conversation.

Ask Open-Ended Questions

Keeping in line with not allowing yourself to give one-word answers, you should try to encourage your conversational partners to do the same. Many conversations come to a screeching halt with single-word answers.

An elaborated answer or a single-word answer followed by a qualifying statement or follow-up question keeps the conversation going. The more details within the response, the more likely you or someone else in the conversation will be able to continue the conversation.

Generally speaking, there are two ways to do this. The first is to ask follow-up questions, and the second is to ask open-ended questions. Asking follow-up questions takes a little bit of skill as it requires you to listen to the answer and develop another question to ask.

The easier option is to ask open-ended questions. Open-ended questions require a sentence or phrase as their answer, as opposed to a simple 'yes' or 'no.' Asking open-ended questions is an easier way to encourage an ongoing conversation as it takes the pressure of developing follow-up questions and comments off of you, especially if you are just learning how to become a better conversationalist.

Show Genuine Interest

However, asking open-ended questions is not enough to be considered a good conversationalist, nor is it enough to encourage the conversation to continue. This is because asking frivolous and unimportant open-ended questions can make you seem as though you are not interested in the conversation. That's why you should focus on questions that fit in the scope of the social situation and show that you are genuinely interested in the response.

For instance, if we use the example of the local business conference with attendees from the same city, if you were to ask someone how their commute was to the conference from their hometown, you would be seen as not being aware of the situation at hand, rather than simply asking a question to ask a question.

Therefore, to be considered a skilled and well-rounded conversationalist, show interest in your conversational partners' responses. By doing so, you will be better equipped to continue the conversation while making the other individual feel comfortable and respected.

Listen

A sixth important quality for a skilled conversationalist is to listen. Don't just listen to the responses given; also listen to the questions others ask and what is being talked about beforehand and in surrounding conversations.

By listening to the responses that your partners give, you will be better equipped to continue the conversation. Furthermore, it is important to listen to what other individuals in the conversation are asking to not ask similar questions. Asking the same question someone else already asked will make you seem uninterested in the conversation.

Lastly, it is important to listen to what individuals are talking about around you. This does not mean you should eavesdrop on other conversations and interrupt them. Instead, it means you should listen to the conversations around you to ensure your conversation fits into the appropriateness of a social event. You do not want to be at a formal social event and talk loudly and wildly about a topic that does not fit in with the social expectation.

Again, not that that's necessarily wrong; after all, if you find a connection with someone, the conversation can naturally flow to a wide variety of topics. Rather, it shows you are aware of your surroundings and respectful of what the other individuals will be talking about.

Allow me to use one more example to further explain this concept. Imagine you are at a somber or serious event such as a funeral. Pending the specifics of the funeral, certain topics of discussion may be considered inappropriate; for example, laughing or giggling at an image or rudely discussing someone's appearance.

Therefore, if you are at a loss for topics of conversation, listen to what other individuals may be talking about, and strike up your own similar conversation with a separate group of people.

Avoid Oversharing

One last trait that is shared among good conversationalists is that they are aware of how much personal information they should share in different situations. Of course, you should answer each question with more than a one-word answer, and you can add a personal story to some of your questions. However, there is a balance required between sharing pertinent information and oversharing.

Oversharing personal details in conversations that do not ask for it can have a few different negative consequences. First, it can make your conversation partners feel uncomfortable; be sure the amount of information shared is proportionate to the situation and the question asked. Another reason that oversharing is not an aspect of good conversation practice is that it makes you seem unaware or unconcerned with your surroundings. There are few social situations and situations in general where sharing your deepest thoughts and feelings is appropriate. Therefore, if you overshare in one of those inappropriate situations, you will be considered inappropriate and disrespectful to the others around you.

* * *

Generally speaking, individuals skilled in the art of conversation are aware of the expectations and requirements of each social situation and show interest in their conversation partners. No matter what questions you ask, as long as they are situationally appropriate and show your audience that you are genuinely interested and concerned with their answers to your questions, you will present yourself as a more attractive and charismatic person (Griffin, 2018).

Now that you have a better understanding of how to become a better conversationalist, it is time to dive into the different sorts of social situations and the specific conversation starters that can be used.

CHAPTER 2

LIGHT AND LOW-PRESSURE CONVERSATIONS

The first collection of conversation starters and possible responses and follow-up questions is meant to ease you into developing a higher level of confidence and conversation skills.

These lighter and low-pressure conversation starters should be used in casual conversation and with either familiar individuals or strangers. Generally, they can be used in any social situation that is low pressure or requires a sense of calm. For instance, these situations can range from friendly group gatherings to casual outings with a mixture of familiar faces and strangers to trying to relax yourself and the other individual on a first date.

These conversation starters are considered light and low pressure as they do not ask a lot for a response. They are entertaining and at times humorous to put the asker and the responder at ease. Additionally, they also have the power to develop the conversation into a larger conversation with little to no effort, making it seem as though you are a talented and skilled conversationalist.

Although these are questions that can be used generally in casual conversation, it is important to make sure that your conversation fits within the scope of your situation. Also, feel free to rephrase the questions to be more casual.

1. Have you gone on any fun outings or to any concerts lately?

    a. Possible response: I went to a great concert the other day/week/month. It was great! But very loud.

        i. Possible follow-up: How many concerts [or events of the same type] have you been to?

2. What is your favorite song to sing in the shower?

    a. Possible response: Anything that makes me sing really loud. Like I'm putting on my own concert.

        i. Possible follow-up: Do you have the talent and courage to sing in front of people?

3. I get so confused when people on television wear shoes in their house. Do you prefer wearing shoes, slippers, socks, or going barefoot at home?

    a. Possible response: I don't wear shoes either! But I do like to keep my feet warm, so I wear slippers.

      i.   Possible follow-up: Do you find that your feet get too hot with slippers on?

4. I just had the most amazing [blank] to eat. Have you eaten anything exceptionally good lately?

    a. Possible response: I tried a donut from the donut shop down the road; it was a new flavor, maple bacon!

      i.   Possible follow-up: Have you ever had a donut that you didn't like?

5. Have you seen some of the crazy hair trends lately? What has been your worst haircut?

    a. Possible response: I had a horrible bowl cut when I was younger! My mother gave it to me.

      i.   Possible follow-up: I think we all had that haircut!

Commiserating over a common experience can build a closer relationship with your partner.

6. Did you hear about [specific celebrity scandal]? What celebrity scandal has stood out to you the most?

    a. Possible response: I'm not really surprised by anything celebrities do anymore. All of the scandals are the same.

      i.   Possible follow-up: Do you think celebrities think they are above or better than the rest of us?

7. Have you ever tried pickles and ice cream? What has been the weirdest food combination that you have tried?

     a. Possible response: I don't know how weird it is but I love putting sugar on my popcorn.

       i. Possible follow-up: Oh yes, that sweet and salty combination always works. How did you start doing that?

Be prepared for weird food combinations with this question. Asking the follow-up of how they discovered it is almost always a safe choice.

8. What is the silliest thing you have ever seen posted online?

     a. Possible response: I can't stand when people constantly post about their significant other! One or two posts are fine or on special days. But every day is too much.

       i. Possible follow-up: It makes it worse when they break up and post about that too and pretend it is no one else's business.

Again, commiserating about a shared opinion can help move the conversation along. However, be prepared that they may find something silly that you do not.

9. Out of all of the crazy fashion trends, which is your least favorite?

     a. Possible response: I don't understand the mixing and matching of patterns. Things match for a reason.

       i. Possible follow-up: Really? You don't think the trend of extremely distressed clothes is worse?

Be careful with this follow-up as you do not want to accidentally say you dislike a trend that they are wearing.

10. What is your favorite restaurant?

 a. Possible response: I love [fill in restaurant here].

 i. Possible follow-up: Oh yes! I love that spot. What is your favorite dish?

11. What is your favorite guilty pleasure TV show?

 a. Possible response: I love all game shows! Especially the old ones or the trivia ones.

 i. Possible follow-up: What do you like about them? Why do you think they aren't mainstream?

12. What is the best or worst piece of advice you have ever been given?

 a. Possible response: I was once told that patience is a skill that sets you apart from all others.

 i. Possible follow-up: When has the advice worked out for you? Who told you that advice?

13. What is the worst/best pickup line you've heard/used?

 a. Possible response: The one I love and hate at the same time is, "Are you a parking ticket? Because you have FINE written all over you."

 i. Possible follow-up: Who has said that to you? Have you used it yourself? Does it work?

14. If you could have dinner with anyone, living or dead, who would it be?

a. Possible response: Kid Rock. I know it's a weird choice, but I think he would be interesting and have some good stories.

   i. Possible follow-up: What would you ask them?

15. If you could only eat one thing for the rest of your life, what would it be?

a. Possible response: Pizza! Hands down, pizza!

   i. Possible follow-up: Why did you pick that?

Simply asking them to elaborate is a trusty and simple follow-up question that works well in this scenario.

16. Are you a cat or a dog person?

a. Possible response: I have both, but I have to say that I love my dog more. Only because he seems to like me more than my cat does.

   i. Possible follow-up: Is there another kind of pet that you would like more?

17. Which celebrity's life would you want to swap with?

a. Possible response: I would love to live as [insert name here].

   i. Possible follow-up: What aspects of their life would you want to avoid?

18. If you could live anywhere in the world, where would it be?

a. Possible response: I love [insert place here]. Their way of living just appeals to me.

      i.   Possible follow-up: Where is one place that you would never want to live?

19. What is the strangest gift you have ever received?

    a.   Possible response: I once received [insert gift name].

      i.   Possible follow-up: Who gave that to you? For what occasion did you receive it? Do you still have it?

20. What has been your favorite compliment to receive?

    a.   Possible response: I love when people compliment my mind or my wit. They are two areas that I work on and am proud of.

      i.   Possible follow-up: Do you have a favorite compliment to give?

21. How did you first hear about this place? [Mention where you are]

    a.   Possible response: I heard of it through a friend.

      i.   Possible follow-up: Do you regularly go to them for recommendations?

22. If you won the lottery, what would be your first big purchase?

    a.   Possible response: A bigger television or a trip somewhere.

      i.   Possible follow-up: Is there an aspect of your life that you would not want to improve?

23. What television series could you not get through?

a. Possible response: I know everyone says that it is worth it, but I cannot get into *Friends* [or insert other television show name here].

    i. Possible follow-up: What made you try to watch it in the first place? Why can't you finish it? Have you tried to watch it multiple times?

24. What television series do you watch over and over again?

a. Possible response: I love *The West Wing* [or insert other television show name here].

    i. Possible follow-up: What do you like about it? What makes you keep coming back? How did you hear about it? What drew you to it the first time?

25. What sporting event can you not stand to watch on television?

a. Possible response: I cannot stand baseball on television or live [or insert other sport here].

    i. Possible follow-up: Why do you not like it? Is it different live? Do you dislike the sport in general?

26. What has been your favorite vacation spot?

a. Possible response: I love just going camping. I don't like fancy vacations.

    i. Possible follow-up: What do you like to do there? How often have you been/are you able to go?

27. If you could change your name, what would you change it to?

a. Possible response: I would probably change it to something crazy and random. Maybe an inanimate object, like celebrities name their children.

    i. Possible follow-up: Why would you change it to that? What do you think names say about us?

28. What part of your daily routine is your favorite?

a. Possible response: Going to sleep. My days are always so busy and filled with events. Don't get me wrong, I love my life, but going to sleep at night after a busy day is amazing.

    i. Possible follow-up: Do you go out of your way to make sure that you stick to your routine? When you miss, skip, or alter that part, how does it throw you off?

29. What is your earliest memory?

a. Possible response: I remember going to an outdoor concert when I was maybe five or six.

    i. Possible follow-up: How does that memory make you feel? How do you think that the memory has changed or affected you?

Everyone's memory will be different. If you cannot think of a specific follow-up question, asking a generalized follow-up will work well.

30. What is the nicest thing anyone has ever done for you?

a. Possible response: [insert experience here; these will range dramatically from person to person]

      i.   Possible follow-up: What do you think made them do that? How did it make you feel? Are you still close to that person? Did you do anything in return?

31. Can you describe yourself in three words?

    a.   Possible response: [the individual will use three words; each person's will be different]

      i.   Possible follow-up: Why did you choose those? Are those values that are important to you? Do you think others would use the same words?

32. If you could change bodies with someone for a day, who would it be and what would be the first thing you'd do?

    a.   Possible response: A model and get dressed. I would love to see how the clothes would fit differently.

      i.   Possible follow-up: How do you think doing that will be different than how you do that now? Can you do that in your body? What appeals to you about their body?

33. What instrument do you play?

    a.   Possible response: I never had the patience to learn how to play an instrument.

      i.   Possible follow-up: What instrument do you wish you could play?

    b.   Possible response: I play the [insert instrument here].

      i.   Possible follow-up: When did you begin to learn how to play? Would you consider yourself good at it? What do you like about playing?

34. Have you ever donated to charity? What made you do it?

    a. Possible response: I've never actually made an official donation. I usually just donate money when I'm asked at a store checkout.

        i. Possible follow-up: Do you think donating money is a positive character trait? Do you think everyone who donates does it for good, or are there alternative motives?

35. What is your biggest accomplishment?

    a. Possible response: [insert achievement]

        i. Possible follow-up: What steps did you take to reach that goal? Has it always been a goal of yours? Did you come across it accidentally, or did you purposefully aim to achieve it?

Again, if you cannot think of a specific follow-up question, general follow-ups will work just as well.

36. Who do you count on the most?

    a. Possible response: My partner. I rely and count on them for so many things like support, friendship, love, etc.

        i. Possible follow-up: Do they know you count on them? Do they fulfill your need for them?

37. What would be your ideal day?

    a. Possible response: [insert details of a perfect day; this may include wake up times, activities during the day, meals, and individuals they see]

        i. Possible follow-up: How is that different from your day-to-day routine?

38. If you could be any animal for a day, what would it be?

    a. Possible response: I would love to be my dog; he has a pretty good life.

        i. Possible follow-up: Why did you choose that animal? Is there any part of their life you would not want to experience? Is there an animal that you would never want to live as, even for a moment?

39. What award has been your favorite to win?

    a. Possible response: I've never actually won an award.

        i. Possible follow-up: What award would you love to win? If you could give yourself an award what would it be for?

    b. Possible response: I've won [insert award name].

        i. Possible follow-up: What did you do to win it? Were you nominated/who nominated you for it?

40. What do you remember to be the most difficult part of being a kid?

    a. Possible response: I never understood why my parents didn't let us eat out more. I didn't see the point of it. I didn't like how I never had the power to make a decision.

    i.   Possible follow-up: Has your opinion changed now that you are older? Was that really a bad thing?

41. What makes you laugh so hard that you can't breathe?

    a.   Possible response: Physical humor! I'm a sucker for people falling down.

    i.   Possible follow-up: What about that makes you laugh so hard?

42. Do you have a cherished family heirloom?

    a.   Possible response: I have a [insert object name here].

    i.   Possible follow-up: Who handed it down to you? What is the story behind it? How long has it been in your family?

43. Do you have many acquaintances or a few close friends?

    a.   Possible response: I have a few close friends.

    i.   Possible follow-up: Was that a purposeful development? Do you wish you had it the other way?

44. Do you prefer chewing gum or having a breath mint?

    a.   Possible response: I would rather have a mint. I can't stand the sound of people chewing.

    i.   Possible follow-up: Is there a brand that you like better than others? Do you use it to relieve bad breath or as just an oral fixation?

45. Do you have a favorite family member?

   a. Possible response: I do. I definitely do. It's my sister/brother/cousin/parent/etc.

      i. Possible follow-up: What sets them apart from the others? Have they always been your favorite?

46. Do you consider yourself a lucky person? Why or why not?

   a. Possible response: Yes/no, [explanation as to why].

      i. Possible follow-up: What would need to happen for you to think differently?

47. Do you consider yourself to be a patient person? Why or why not?

   a. Possible response: At times. I think it really depends on the situation.

      i. Possible follow-up: In what situations are you patient or not patient? Do you have a weakness for one specific thing that breaks your nerve?

48. Do you have a favorite or least favorite genre of movies or television shows?

   a. Possible response: I don't like bad movies, like really slow movies. I need things to happen.

      i. Possible follow-up: What about them don't you like? What do you think has made you or influenced you to feel this way?

49. Did you have an ideal career when you were younger?

a. Possible response: I wanted to be everything. I think I changed my mind every week.

    i. Possible follow-up: What about the different jobs appealed to you? How does your current position hold up to your childhood dreams? Did you ever think you would become what you wanted to be as a child?

50. What is one product that you cannot live without?

a. Possible response: I have this one hair clip/face wash/coffee mug/etc. that is really special to me. I would be lost without it.

    i. Possible follow-up: What about it makes it so special? Was it always special and necessary to you? Where did you get it?

CHAPTER 3

BUSINESS AND FORMAL CONVERSATION

The second collection of conversation topics and starters is meant to be used in business and more formal situations, essentially any situation where manners and higher levels of etiquette are expected. This means that these starters and topics can be used for business socials, networking events, speaking to individuals of authority, or in group conference settings.

In these situations, conversations should not be too intrusive for the other individuals, allow for collaboration, and build professional relationships and connections between yourself and others.

To thrive in these more formal conversations, you want to present yourself as confident and as a conversationalist who is aware of the expectations and conventions associated with the situation. In the end, being a strong conversationalist in business and formal situations will make others feel more confident in your professional abilities and make you a more valuable member of their team.

1. How did you hear about this event?

   a. Possible response: I heard about it through my work bulletin board. They are always posting about these kinds of events.

      i. Possible follow-up: What other kinds of events like that have you been to?

2. What was the first job you ever had?

   a. Possible response: I had a few. I was a babysitter and paperboy at first, I think. Then I went on to be a cashier at a grocery store.

      i. Possible follow-up: Do you think they prepared you in any way for the job you have now? What kind of skills did they allow you to develop?

3. What's a good place to eat around here on a lunch break?

   a. Possible response: [insert name of suggestion]

      i. Possible follow-up: Thank you; that is so helpful! What do you like about it? Any specific dishes I should try? Can you draw me a map to get to it?

4. Are there any books that one can read to better understand your job?

   a. Possible response: Yes, there is a great one called [insert book title here].

      i. Possible follow-up: Have you read it? What did you learn from it?

      b. Possible response: No, I don't believe that there are.

          i.   Possible follow-up: Have you ever read a book to prepare you for any job or position?

5. What are you reading right now?

      a. Possible response: [insert response here]

          i.   Possible follow-up: Are you liking it? Is it something you would recommend? What is good or bad about it? If you could, do you have any suggestions for the author?

      b. Possible response: No, I don't really read that much.

          i.   Possible follow-up: Is there a book from your past that has stuck with you? Do you simply not have time, or do you not like reading?

6. How was your commute here? [If the meeting is not at their place of employment.]

      a. Possible response: It was okay. I took the [insert directions or specific method of commute].

          i.   Possible follow-up: How does it compare to your commute to work?

7. How do you ensure you have fun on the weekends?

      a. Possible response: I try to leave my work at work. That way I can focus on my family. The weekend gets pretty busy with family things.

          i.   Possible follow-up: I can imagine your family being very appreciative of that! Do you find it hard to go back to work on Monday?

8. How do you make sure you do not bring work home?

   a. Possible response: [The individual will most likely respond with an answer about working hard and staying focused.]

      i. Possible follow-up: How did you develop that technique and philosophy? How well does it work for you?

9. Does your profession encourage you to go to conferences? Which have you attended?

   a. Possible response: It does, but it is not a job requirement. I have been to [list conferences].

      i. Possible follow-up: Do you think they have made you a better employee? Do you believe that they are beneficial?

10. How long have you been at your current job or in your current position?

    a. Possible response: I have held this position for about three years now.

       i. Possible follow-up: How did you come to hold your job? Did you get a promotion? Did you quit another job?

11. What's the most interesting project/contract/job that you have ever worked on?

    a. Possible response: There was this one job I had where [insert details about the job].

       i.   Possible follow-up: What did you find interesting about it? Do you get a lot of projects like that? Were you able to work in a group?

12. Where do you see yourself in five years in relation to your job/employment position?

    a. Possible response: I hope to be in a high position within the same company, maybe with a pay raise too.

       i.   Possible follow-up: Is it the same place you have always seen yourself? How has your future picture of yourself changed over the years?

13. Have you ever won an award for your work?

    a. Possible response: I have. It was for [insert reason].

       i.   Possible follow-up: How often is that award given out? Who nominated you?

    b. Possible response: Unfortunately, no, I haven't.

       i.   Possible follow-up: If you could give yourself an award for your work, what would it be for?

14. How old were you when you had your first job? What was it?

    a. Possible response: I was 13 years old. I was a paperboy for my neighborhood.

       i.   Possible follow-up: Did you enjoy it? How did you get the job?

15. What do you think is your strongest sense?

a. Possible response: My sense of intuition, I think. I can predict certain things before they happen and react accordingly.

   i. Possible follow-up: How did you develop that sense? Do others know you as having such a good sense of [repeat whatever sense they said]?

16. If you were told that you were not able to fail, what would you try to do?

a. Possible response: I would ask for a raise or make some suggestions that I've been afraid of doing.

   i. Possible follow-up: What is stopping you from doing those things now?

17. If you could give one piece of advice to pass on to the next generation or newer employees at your job, what would it be?

a. Possible response: Be patient. There is a lot of room to grow once you've been here for a year or two.

   i. Possible follow-up: Do you think that piece of advice fits with other jobs or positions of employment? Did someone share that with you when you first started?

18. If you could hang a motto in every place of work, what would it say?

a. Possible response: [insert motto]

   i. Possible follow-up: Why do you like that motto? Is there a workplace motto that you are sick of seeing?

19. What do you think success means in your job?

    a. Possible response: I think success is being happy in this job and having a good client base that trusts you.

        i. Possible follow-up: Do you think that it can translate to success in life in general? Do you believe you are on track to become successful?

20. Why is it important to set personal goals?

    a. Possible response: I think it is important because external motivation isn't enough.

        i. Possible follow-up: What are some personal goals for your job that you have set? How do you ensure you reach them?

21. What do you think is the secret to a long, successful employment?

    a. Possible response: Knowing when to stay quiet and when to speak up.

        i. Possible follow-up: Do you embody this advice?

22. Do you think it is better to ask for permission or forgiveness at work?

    a. Possible response: I think it depends on the situation and the possible consequences of your actions.

        i. Possible follow-up: Can you share an example?

23. What does it mean to be powerful in your line of work?

a. Possible response: I think the most powerful people in my line of work are those individuals who are trusted and looked up to by others.

    i. Possible follow-up: Can you give me an example of someone in your company? Do you think you are on track to becoming powerful?

24. What's the best method of conflict resolution at your job?

a. Possible response: I'm not too sure. I think facing the issue head-on is always beneficial.

    i. Possible follow-up: How and why did you develop that philosophy? Have you had to resolve any conflicts in your position?

25. Which holds more weight and importance: what you say or how you say it?

a. Possible response: Again, I think it depends on your message. What are you trying to communicate?

    i. Possible follow-up: When has your message been changed by how you've said something?

26. Which do you think is more important, the end product or how you got there?

a. Possible response: I think how you get there is more important. The end goal is expected; the path to get there is up to you.

    i. Possible follow-up: How have you developed this belief? Can you think of a project where the opposite is true?

27. Is it ever acceptable to make a threat? Is a threat always a threat?

    a. Possible response: I think that threats are dangerous. Even if you don't mean them to be threatening, they can have some rather adverse effects.

        i. Possible follow-up: Do you have personal experience that has allowed you to develop this belief?

28. What role does trust play in your everyday job and duties?

    a. Possible response: I have a large client base that puts their trust in me to [insert role and responsibility].

        i. Possible follow-up: How do you uphold that responsibility and role?

29. What's the best way to earn another person's respect in general and in your position?

    a. Possible response: Just be honest and follow through with what you say; back up your words with actions.

        i. Possible follow-up: Do you think you embody this advice? Are there many people in your job that you respect for this reason?

30. Have you ever negotiated a raise for yourself? What is the best way to go about doing that?

    a. Possible response: I never have; I've been too scared.

        i. Possible follow-up: What specifically has stopped you?

b. Possible response: I have. The best way is [insert advice].

  i. Possible follow-up: What advice would you give to someone who wants to negotiate a raise?

31. What is the difference between helping people and showing them how to help themselves? Is one more important than the other?

a. Possible response: I believe you need to strike a balance between the two.

  i. Possible follow-up: Can you give me an example of when you helped someone and when you showed someone how to help themselves?

32. How do you measure happiness in your job?

a. Possible response: I think happiness is measured by how I feel going into work. Do I feel excited? Or do I dread it?

  i. Possible follow-up: Do you think the same standard can be applied to life in general?

33. What do you believe is the best way to deal with and handle the lack of performance or effort from coworkers?

a. Possible response: Just like conflict, I think respectfully confronting them is the best way to start.

  i. Possible follow-up: Have you ever had to deal with employees who do less work?

34. How important is dressing properly for your job? Is there great importance placed on physical appearance?

   a. Possible response: Well, the way you dress presents how qualified you are for the job. For example, we have a dress code at the office.

      i. Possible follow-up: If you had no dress code, would you still want to dress the same way for your job? Is there any part of the dress code that you would change?

35. When a mistake is made, does it matter whether or not it was done intentionally?

   a. Possible response: I don't think it matters if it's done intentionally. I think it's important to take responsibility for any mistake you make.

      i. Possible follow-up: Have you ever made a mistake that you didn't want to take responsibility for?

36. What have you found to be the best method of reducing different kinds of anxiety at work? Such as performance and presentation anxiety?

   a. Possible response: Practice. I practice presentations a lot before I give them. You can also ask coworkers for support.

      i. Possible follow-up: Do you apply the same anxiety-reducing practices to life in general?

37. Do you believe failure is always a bad thing?

   a. Possible response: It's only bad if you let it discourage you.

     i.   Possible follow-up: Have you had a setback or failure that has stuck with you over the years?

38. How do you productively handle your frustrations at work?

    a.   Possible response: I try to turn them into inspiration. There has to be a problem that brought about the frustration, so I try to solve the problem.

        i.   Possible follow-up: Can you give me an example of how you have done that in the past?

39. What about your job do you find stresses you out?

    a.   Possible response: There is a lot actually. [The individual will then list their possible stresses at work.]

        i.   Possible follow-up: How do you work to lessen those stresses?

40. What is something about your job that always brings a smile to your face?

    a.   Possible response: I like the people; my coworkers are a great group of people.

        i.   Possible follow-up: Are you friends with them outside of work? Is that the same aspect of other jobs that you've liked as well?

41. Have you been to this conference/networking event before?

    a.   Possible response: I haven't.

        i.   Possible follow-up: Are you enjoying yourself?

    b.   Possible response: I have, yes, a few times.

        i.   Possible follow-up: What brings you back every time?

42. Who did you come with to this conference/networking event?

    a.   Possible response: I came with my coworkers.

        i.   Possible follow-up: Are you learning some good interpersonal strategies together?

43. Are there similar events that you recommend?

    a.   Possible response: Yes, [individual may list other events].

        i.   Possible follow-up: Can you give me some details about those events?

44. Do you work in the area?

    a.   Possible response: I do. I work [describes the area where they work].

        i.   Possible follow-up: Do you like that location?

    b.   Possible response: I don't; I work out of town.

        i.   Possible follow-up: What brought you to this event so far away?

45. What about this event interested you?

    a.   Possible response: I like that it includes [list of reasons].

        i.   Possible follow-up: Are you generally drawn to events that include [repeat what individual said]?

46. What about your job keeps you the busiest?

a. Possible response: [The individual will likely make a list of aspects of their job.]

    i. Possible follow-up: How do you balance the busyness?

47. I'm trying to decide which panel to attend next; do you have any suggestions?

a. Possible response: I've heard that [blank] is a great speaker.

    i. Possible follow-up: Have you heard them speak before? What do you think about this [blank] panel/speaker?

48. I'm new to these types of events; how does this event compare to the others you have been to?

a. Possible response: It is pretty good/not very good.

    i. Possible follow-up: Can you suggest other events like it? Can you suggest better events?

49. Do you come to a lot of these types of events? Do you find they are helpful?

a. Possible response: It depends on what you are looking for. Just like everything, you get out what you put in.

    i. Possible follow-up: What is one piece of advice or benefit you have taken from these types of events? How do you ensure you make these events worth it?

50. I am not from around here; do you know any good restaurants?

a. Possible response: [insert recommendation]

i. Possible follow-up: Can you give me directions? Do you have any suggestions for dishes to order?

CHAPTER 4

QUESTIONS OF PREFERENCE AND MISCELLANEOUS CONVERSATIONS

The third collection of conversation starters is for miscellaneous conversations. Not every social situation has a cut-and-dry or explicit set of expectations. For this reason, it can be useful to have a few low-pressure yet still interesting conversation starters at your disposal that can help bring any conversation back to life.

Conversation starters that deal with preference are usually a safe bet as they ask the other individual about a random preference of theirs. Their answer can then be used as a springboard into another topic. Of course, as long as the question remains unintrusive.

Unlike the three other chapters that deal with specific situations, these miscellaneous questions can be used to liven up any conversation and in a combination of one or more of the described situations. For example, these questions can be used in casual and formal situations. For this reason, they were given their own chapter.

1. How long can you go without checking your phone?

    a. Possible response: Only a few hours, I think. I use it a lot to help with boredom.

        i. Possible follow-up: Do you think people rely on their phones too much? Would it be hard for you to have a phone-free day?

2. Have you ever kept a New Year's Resolution? What was it?

    a. Possible response: I have. It was [insert resolution].

        i. Possible follow-up: What made you successful?

    b. Possible response: I haven't yet.

        i. Possible follow-up: What has made you fail?

3. What bad habit do you wish you could break?

    a. Possible response: I wish to break [insert habit].

        i. Possible follow-up: What is stopping you from breaking the habit? How did you develop the habit?

4. Do you have a morning or daily routine? What does it include?

    a. Possible response: I do. I always do [list steps of routine].

  i. Possible follow-up: Do you enjoy your routine? Do you wish you could change it in any way? Do you find your routine productive?

5. Are you able to tell when someone is hiding something from you?

  a. Possible response: I can!

    i. Possible follow-up: What are your tricks to do so?

6. What is your favorite vintage object that you wish would come back in style?

  a. Possible response: I wish old shoes would come back in style. You can't find them anywhere.

    i. Possible follow-up: What about them do you like better than their modern-day counterparts?

7. Do you have a hero or role model? Who is it?

  a. Possible response: I do; I look up to [insert name].

    i. Possible follow-up: Why do you look up to them? Do they know they are your role model? Have you ever met them? Have they ever let you down?

8. Have you ever had your fortune told? Would you ever consider it?

  a. Possible response: I have! I didn't take it seriously, though.

i. Possible follow-up: Do you believe that it will come true? What made you get your fortune told?

9. Which social media app can you not live without?

a. Possible response: I love [insert preferred app].

i. Possible follow-up: What do you like about it? Would you change anything about it to make it better? What app do you dislike the most?

10. Which fictional character do you see yourself in?

a. Possible response: I like [insert name of character].

i. Possible follow-up: What about them do you like? What character do you not see yourself in at all? Do you like that character? Do you think others would agree with you?

11. If you were on death row, what would you choose to be your last meal?

a. Possible response: I would choose steak and lobster. And every possible side.

i. Possible follow-up: Is that your favorite meal? Do you have an emotional connection to that meal?

12. What is one piece of advice you wish you knew when you were younger?

a. Possible response: That your attitude counts for everything.

      i.   Possible follow-up: How did you learn that? How do you think that would have helped you in your life growing up?

13. What would you title your memoir if you wrote one?

    a.   Possible response: I would call it [insert name].

      i.   Possible follow-up: Why would you choose that? Would you want to write it yourself? Would it be a tell-all, or are there areas that you would leave out?

14. Do you have any guilty pleasures?

    a.   Possible response: Oh yes! They are [insert answer, which can be almost anything].

      i.   Possible follow-up: What do you think your guilty pleasure says about you? When do you indulge?

15. What is the oddest situation you've found yourself in?

    a.   Possible response: Well, there was this one time [be prepared for odd answers].

      i.   Possible follow-up: How did you handle it? What brought you to the situation?

16. If you were in a band, what would you be called?

    a.   Possible response: I'm not sure. Maybe the [insert name]. [Remember creative questions will vary a lot in their answers.]

i. Possible follow-up: What member would you be? What instrument would you play? What kind of band would it be?

17. What do you find incredibly boring?

a. Possible response: I think reading is boring. I just can't do it.

i. Possible follow-up: Why do you find it boring? Have you always found it boring?

18. Do you have a theme song?

a. Possible response: I would love to steal the theme song from the television show [insert name].

i. Possible follow-up: What about that song fits your life?

19. What alcohol/drink/food item can you not stand?

a. Possible response: I cannot stand Jagermeister. It does not sit well with me.

i. Possible follow-up: Have you always disliked it, or is there a specific negative experience that you associate with it?

20. What popular song is overplayed?

a. Possible response: I think anything by Taylor Swift is overplayed. The problem is that her songs are so catchy.

i. Possible follow-up: Did you like the song the first time you heard it, or have you always disliked it?

21. What is your deal breaker on a first date?

    a. Possible response: Showing up looking unclean or disheveled.

        i. Possible follow-up: Can you forgive any reason for doing that? Do you have a funny story associated with that?

22. When you enter a social gathering, do you like to be the center of attention, or do you like to slip in unnoticed?

    a. Possible response: I don't mind it when people notice me when I walk in, but I don't do it on purpose.

        i. Possible follow-up: Do you think that people who are the center of attention do it forcefully?

23. Are you a sweet, sour, or savory person?

    a. Possible response: I definitely lean more toward the savory side, but I do like all foods.

        i. Possible follow-up: What is your favorite [repeat their answer] food? Do you have any favorite combinations of food pairings?

24. Have you read anything interesting lately?

    a. Possible response: I have. It was a book/magazine article about [insert topic here].

        i. Possible follow-up: Are you usually drawn to books or articles about that topic? How did you come across this book? Would you recommend it?

25. What do you like to do that makes time fly?

a. Possible response: Whenever I'm with friends, time just flies.

    i. Possible follow-up: In those situations, do you sometimes wish time would slow down? What about that situation makes time pass more quickly?

26. What story, real or made up, has stuck with you over the years?

a. Possible response: There is a story from my childhood about [insert title or subject of story].

    i. Possible follow-up: I've never heard that story. What is it about? What about that story has stuck with you? Has it influenced you or affected you in any way that you notice today?

27. Which do you prefer to watch, the sunrise or the sunset?

a. Possible response: I prefer to watch the sunset, mostly because I refuse to wake up early enough to watch the sunrise.

    i. Possible follow-up: Do you think there is something aesthetically different between the sunrise and sunset?

28. Do you like to exercise?

a. Possible response: I don't like to exercise, but I still do it.

    i. Possible follow-up: What pushes you to exercise? Do you have a favorite routine?

29. If you put a bumper sticker on your car that could say anything, what would it be?

    a. Possible response: I love bumper stickers. The more ridiculous the better. Mine would probably say something like, "If you can read this...I'm not impressed. Most people can read."

        i. Possible follow-up: Have you ever seen a bumper sticker that you don't like? What has been the most annoying or ridiculous bumper sticker you have ever seen?

30. Do you consider yourself to be spontaneous? Or does it scare you?

    a. Possible response: I would like to think that I'm spontaneous, but I definitely like to know what's coming.

        i. Possible follow-up: What methods do you have to prepare for the future? In what ways do you wish you were more spontaneous/more scheduled?

31. How do you feel about people who speak loudly about their beliefs?

    a. Possible response: I don't mind them. Unless they are judgmental about other individuals.

        i. Possible follow-up: Have you ever been outspoken about a specific belief?

32. Is there anything that bothers you when it is out of place?

a.   Possible response: I am attached to my daily routine. If an aspect of that is out of place, I feel a little off for the whole day.

    i.   Possible follow-up: What about that makes you uncomfortable when it is out of place?

33. What is your version of a fancy dinner?

a.   Possible response: My version of a fancy dinner is anything that takes multiple steps to prepare. And many hours.

    i.   Possible follow-up: What has been the fanciest dinner you have ever made? What has been the fanciest dinner you have ever eaten? Do you prefer fancy food or simple comfort foods?

34. Would you rather wear a ball gown or sweatpants?

a.   Possible response: I can appreciate a ball gown, but I would much rather be in sweatpants.

    i.   Possible follow-up: Is being comfortable with how you dress more important than being fashionable?

35. What has been the absolute worst movie you have ever seen?

a.   Possible response: The absolute worst movie I have ever seen has to be [insert name of movie].

    i.   Possible follow-up: What about the movie did you not like? Were there any redeeming qualities? What drew you to the movie in the first place?

36. Do you prefer to drive or be driven?

    a.   Possible response: I like to drive because I like being in control of where we're going.

        i.   Possible follow-up: How do you react when you get lost while driving? Do you ask for directions, or would you rather figure it out for yourself?

37. Do you have a favorite season?

    a.   Possible response: My favorite season would have to be [insert season].

        i.   Possible follow-up: If one season had to go, which would it be? What is your favorite memory associated with your favorite season?

38. When you're trying to focus, does it have to be completely quiet, or do you need music?

    a.   Possible response: It depends on what I'm trying to do. Sometimes distractions such as music can help me focus on my task.

        i.   Possible follow-up: Do you have a specific music playlist that you listen to when you are trying to focus?

39. What is your favorite/least favorite saying?

    a.   Possible response: My least favorite saying would have to be one that is incredibly cheesy or over said.

        i.   Possible follow-up: What about that saying do you dislike? Do you focus on your favorite saying to help motivate you?

40. When traveling, do you prefer the window or the aisle seat?

a. Possible response: I prefer the window seat. I like to see where I'm going.

    i. Possible follow-up: What about when you're in an auditorium or concert? Is it the same preference?

41. Do you have a favorite sleep position?

a. Possible response: I usually fall asleep on my side, but I toss and turn throughout the night, so I never wake up in the same position.

    i. Possible follow-up: Do you wish you had a better sleep routine? Have your sleeping habits always been the same?

42. Who in your life are you most proud of?

a. Possible response: I would have to say that I am most proud of my child/sibling/parent/friend/etc.

    i. Possible follow-up: What about them makes you proud of them? Does your pride in them motivate you in any way? Do they know that you are proud of them?

43. What is your most cherished birthday gift or gift in general?

a. Possible response: My most cherished gift would have to be a [insert answer].

    i. Possible follow-up: Who gave you that gift? What about it is special to you? Has it always been special to you, or have you only realized its importance over the years?

44. Have you ever had horrible customer service? What was the situation?

    a. Possible response: I think everyone at one time or another has experienced horrible customer service. My specific horrible experience was [insert details of horrible customer service].

        i. Possible follow-up: Did you previously have good customer service at that establishment? Have you returned to that establishment since?

45. Do you like to keep photographs?

    a. Possible response: I like to keep photographs, but I hardly ever look at them.

        i. Possible follow-up: In your opinion, what is the best way to keep photographs?

46. Have you ever needed to go to the hospital for an injury?

    a. Possible response: Thankfully, I've never had to go to the hospital for myself.

        i. Possible follow-up: Wow, you're lucky! Have you ever had to go to the hospital for someone else?

    b. Possible response: Yes, I was injured when I was a child.

        i. Possible follow-up: What happened? Do you still experience symptoms or effects from your injury?

47. If you could get rid of one negative aspect of your life, what would it be?

a.   Possible response: I'm not a fan of how I procrastinate so much.

    i.   Possible follow-up: How would you get rid of it? What is stopping you from getting rid of that negative aspect?

48. What is your ideal superpower?

a.   Possible response: I would love to be able to tell what other people are thinking. Or turn back time.

    i.   Possible follow-up: How would you use your superpower for good? Do you think you would let your superpower go to your head? How do you think you would take advantage of your superpower?

49. If you could spend your day doing whatever you wanted with no negative consequences, what would you do?

a.   Possible response: I would try to do anything that I've been afraid to do. I would just try to make myself as happy as possible.

    i.   Possible follow-up: What is stopping you from doing those things now?

50. What smell or sound calms you down?

a.   Possible response: Growing up, I loved the smell of my grandmother's kitchen. There was always something delicious cooking, and it always made me feel so happy.

    i.   Possible follow-up: Do you experience that smell in your life now?

CHAPTER 5

DEEPER CONVERSATIONS

The fourth and last collection of conversation starters and topics encourages and ignites a deeper level of conversation. Learning when the situation requires a lighter conversation and when the conversation can handle a deeper level of conversation and asking the questions that bring the conversation deeper is an important part of being a good conversationalist.

Talking about specific topics with others can develop higher levels of intimacy and closeness. This means that these deeper conversation topics are meant to be used in situations ranging from trying to learn more about a new romantic partner with whom you are trying to create a deeper connection to strengthening a friendship. These conversation topics facilitate this type of reaction as they require more honesty and vulnerability from the other person and are less superficial in their subject matter. By answering the questions, your partner provides you with a glimpse into who they are as a person, where they came from, and where they want to go.

These conversation topics should be used carefully as they can come across as intrusive or make the individual uncomfortable. For this reason, it is important to feel comfortable in the conversation yourself. If you feel uncomfortable asking the question or are fearful of the potential answer, then it is, perhaps, not a good idea to ask it.

1. If you could be reincarnated as anything, what would you choose?

    a. Possible response: I would like to be reincarnated as another person. That way I can try to live a different life.

        i. Possible follow-up: Is there anything that you would not want to be reincarnated as?

2. Do you believe in God?

    a. Possible response: I'm not sure if I believe in God. I believe that there might be a larger power that helps and influences our world.

        i. Possible follow-up: What has led you to this belief? Have you always believed this?

3. What life events have made you question your belief?

    a. Possible response: [Be prepared for the individual to name a perhaps unsettling experience.]

        i. Possible follow-up: What was your belief before these life events?

4. What is something that you need to rid yourself of but cannot?

    a. Possible response: I need to get rid of the negative judgments I have about myself.

       i.   Possible follow-up: What is stopping you from ridding yourself of them? Why do you consider them to be a negative aspect of your life?

5. Do you believe you know how you will die?

    a. Possible response: I have absolutely no idea. And I don't really want to talk about it.

       i.   Possible follow-up: Of course.

Be aware that if an individual outwardly says that they do not feel comfortable talking about a subject, it is your responsibility to be respectful and not ask any further questions.

6. Are there any experiences you want to have before you die?

    a. Possible response: Of course! There are some milestones in my job that I want to reach and some vacation experiences as well.

       i.   Possible follow-up: Do you believe you are on track to experiencing them?

7. Are you afraid of dying?

    a. Possible response: I definitely am.

       i.   Possible follow-up: What about it frightens you?

8. What has been the lowest or highest point in your life?

    a. Possible response: The lowest point in my life would have to be [be prepared for the answer to be a little unsettling if the individual speaks about their lowest point].

      i.   Possible follow-up: What aspects of your life helped you out of this low point? How did you move past it? What life choices and events led you to your high point?

9. Have you ever broken a law?

   a. Possible response: I never have.

      i.   Possible follow-up: What is stopping you from breaking the law? Do you agree with most of the laws?

10. If you could see into the future, what would you be most afraid to see?

   a. Possible response: I would most likely be afraid of not being happy in the future.

      i.   Possible follow-up: What do you think you can do now to ensure that your feared future possibility will never happen?

11. Are you happy with your life?

   a. Possible response: I am relatively happy with my life, although there are areas where I'm sure I can improve.

      i.   Possible follow-up: In what areas can you improve? What about your life makes you happy with it? Have you always been happy with your life?

12. Who has let you down the most in your life?

   a. Possible response: I think I've let myself down the most in life.

> i. Possible follow-up: In what ways were you let down? Have you/they been able to redeem themselves in your eyes?

13. Do you consider yourself to have a good support system?

    a. Possible response: I definitely have a good support system. They're always there when I need help without question or judgment.

        i. Possible follow-up: Have you always had such a strong support system? How did you develop your system? Can you tell me specific examples of how they were there for you?

14. Can you think of a time where you were the happiest?

    a. Possible response: I was perhaps the happiest when [insert experience].

        i. Possible follow-up: Did you know at the time that moment was going to be special?

15. Do you believe your priorities and values in life are in line with most people's?

    a. Possible response: I think that my priorities are similar to others.

        i. Possible follow-up: Is it important for you to have others approve of your priorities and values?

16. What do you dislike most about yourself?

    a. Possible response: I don't like how I base my happiness on other people.

        i.   Possible follow-up: When did you realize that you didn't like this about yourself? Have you always had the same insecurities?

17. Do you consider yourself a moral person?

    a. Possible response: I do believe myself to be a moral person. Of course, morality is a tough issue to embody.

        i.   Possible follow-up: Do you abide by a specific moral system or code? Do you think that morality is a universal concept that can be applied, or is it more subjective?

18. What is the most difficult thing you have ever done?

    a. Possible response: The most difficult thing I've ever done was facing my fears.

        i.   Possible follow-up: What brought you to this situation? Did you know that this was going to be a difficult task before entering into the situation? Did the difficult situation provide you an opportunity to learn something or improve yourself?

19. What keeps you up at night worrying?

    a. Possible response: I worry about quite a few things. Most often, I worry about what the next day will bring.

        i.   Possible follow-up: Do you have any coping mechanisms to help you overcome your anxiety and worry? Have you always had this worry, or has it developed through different experiences?

20. Do you trust people easily?

a. Possible response: I used to. For me, trust is something that must be earned.

    i. Possible follow-up: What experiences have led you to this philosophy on trust?

21. What makes you uncomfortable?

a. Possible response: Social outings make me uncomfortable.

    i. Possible follow-up: What about them makes you uncomfortable? Do you have different coping mechanisms to not allow these aspects to take over or hinder your life?

22. Do you think you are too serious or too flippant?

a. Possible response: I think I may be a little too serious in certain situations.

    i. Possible follow-up: How do you think you can strike up a better balance between being serious and easygoing?

23. What relationship do you regret losing/ending?

a. Possible response: I think one relationship that I regret losing is [answers will vary from intimate relationships to friendships to work connections].

    i. Possible follow-up: What about the relationship do you miss? What made you end the relationship in the first place? Do you genuinely miss the relationship or just the good parts of it?

24. What arc you most insecure about?

a. Possible response: I am most insecure about my ability to talk to others. I do not believe my skill is on par with other individuals.

    i. Possible follow-up: Are you taking steps to make yourself more confident in that area?

25. Is there a part of you that wishes you could change in a certain way?

a. Possible response: I wish I could change [the answer will vary from something superficial to something a little bit more personal. Although this question is meant to be personal, do not be offended or pry if the answer is more superficial than you would have liked].

    i. Possible follow-up: What is it about that part of you that you wish to change? Is it possible to change bad things about yourself, or are they something you have to learn to live with?

26. Do you avoid or thrive in conflict?

a. Possible response: I love drama and conflict. It is a guilty pleasure of mine.

    i. Possible follow-up: What about conflict makes you avoid it or draws you to it? Is there a specific type of drama or conflict that you are drawn to more than others? Does your opinion change when it is conflict that involves you?

27. Are you a leader or a follower?

a. Possible response: I would like to think that I am a leader, but I am more of a follower.

      i.   Possible follow-up: What aspects of your personality do you believe influence this decision? Are you happy with your place, or do you wish to be more of the latter?

28. Do you like to follow or break rules?

    a.   Possible response: I think rules are there for a reason, and I try to abide by them as much as possible.

      i.   Possible follow-up: Do you think rules limit individuals or allow them to be free within them?

29. Are there any laws or rules that you believe you are exempt from?

    a.   Possible response: It depends on the situation.

      i.   Possible follow-up: Can you give me an example of a specific situation and rule that you believe you are exempt from? Why do you believe you should have special treatment?

30. What goal or dreams do you have that you believe are unrealistic?

    a.   Possible response: I have always wanted to [insert dream].

      i.   Possible follow-up: What about this dream makes you believe that it is unrealistic? Have you ever tried to achieve it?

31. What challenge has really pushed you and tested your limits and abilities?

      a. Possible response: Trying to figure out what I wanted to do with my life has been probably the biggest challenge so far.

          i. Possible follow-up: In what ways did you help yourself cope with the stresses? Is it a challenge that you are proud of working through? Are you happy with the results?

32. Is there a hobby or skill you wish you had?

      a. Possible response: I simply wish I had hobbies in general. I do not have the time.

          i. Possible follow-up: What is stopping you from developing the hobby or the skill? Have you always wanted to develop the hobby? Are you afraid of failing, which is why you are not making the time to develop a hobby?

33. What is your biggest regret in life?

      a. Possible response: I don't necessarily believe in regrets, but there was this one time that I keep thinking about [state specific experience].

          i. Possible follow-up: Do you think that the outcome of that experience has influenced you in any sort of positive way? How do you think your life would be different if that regretful situation had been different?

34. Do you think your parents did a good job raising you?

      a. Possible response: I think my parents did a good job in preparing me for the world. Although at the time, I did not really agree with them.

i. Possible follow-up: What aspect of your parent's child-rearing skills has stuck with you the most?

35. What about adulthood are you disappointed in?

a. Possible response: I was not prepared for all of the responsibilities. Not necessarily the tasks but having to take responsibility for different things.

i. Possible follow-up: What have you done to counteract and cope with this disappointment?

36. Are you afraid people will judge you?

a. Possible response: I am. But I try to not care about what other people think.

i. Possible follow-up: What about you do you feel people judge the most?

37. What do you find you daydream about most?

a. Possible response: I daydream about having time to myself.

i. Possible follow-up: What aspects of your life can you change to make your daydream a reality?

38. Do you like your job?

a. Possible response: I enjoy aspects of my job; however, the job in its entirety can be stressful.

i. Possible follow-up: Is the job what you thought it was going to be? Is it a job that you thought you would hold as a child?

39. Are you overly competitive?

    a. Possible response: I do find that I am rather competitive in certain aspects and areas of my life.

        i. Possible follow-up: Do you think your competitive nature, or lack thereof, has influenced your life in any way? Can you give me specific examples?

40. Do you enjoy being the center of attention?

    a. Possible response: It depends on the situation. If I'm the center of attention on my birthday, that's one thing, but being the center of attention for something negative is totally different.

        i. Possible follow-up: Do you act differently when you are the center of attention?

41. Do you think you are good with your money?

    a. Possible response: I believe that I am okay with my money. I do enjoy splurging and spoiling myself at certain times.

        i. Possible follow-up: How do you think you can improve your money-spending skills? Where did you learn the value of a dollar from?

42. What inspires you?

    a. Possible response: I try to inspire myself as much as possible, but most of my inspiration comes from other people.

        i. Possible follow-up: Are you inspired easily? Do you get discouraged easily? Do you have specific individuals in your life who inspire you more than others?

43. Are you a people-pleaser?

    a. Possible response: I do enjoy pleasing people. But I do try to make sure that I keep my integrity while doing so.

        i. Possible follow-up: Do you base your importance and value on the happiness of other people? Have you ever compromised your own values and integrity to please another person?

44. Does your age bother you? Does getting older make you nervous?

    a. Possible response: My specific age doesn't bother me. But the general idea of getting older makes me a little nervous.

        i. Possible follow-up: Do you have an age that you are afraid to hit? What about the aging process makes you nervous? When growing up, did you have adults that were also worried about aging?

45. Who is the first person you call when you have good news?

    a. Possible response: I think that might depend on what kind of good news it is, but generally, I would probably call my significant other first.

        i. Possible follow-up: What about that person makes you want to call them first?

46. When do you feel most like yourself?

    a. Possible response: I feel the most like myself when I am [insert specific experience or skill].

        i. Possible follow-up: What about that makes you feel comfortable? Have you always favored that activity?

47. Do you get caught up in world news, or do you enjoy being blissfully unaware?

    a. Possible response: I want to be somewhat up to date with what is going on. It really depends on how disturbing the news is.

        i. Possible follow-up: Do you think there is a benefit to being blissfully unaware of what is going on in the world?

48. What are you most afraid of?

    a. Possible response: I'm most afraid of being unhappy in my life.

        i. Possible follow-up: In what ways are you working to ensure that you do not face this fear?

49. Are you on track to achieve some of your goals?

    a. Possible response: I think I am. But I'm sure I have a long way to go.

        i. Possible follow-up: What goals do you believe you will reach first? Do you have a priority of which ones you want to achieve more than others? Do you have any goals that you think you will never achieve?

50. Are there any situations that make you shy?

    a. Possible response: I'm not generally a shy person. But if I am in a group of individuals who I don't know and I do not have time to mentally prepare for the task or event, then I do find myself to be a little shy.

        i. Possible follow-up: In what ways do you help yourself overcome your shyness?

CONCLUSION

Being a good conversationalist does not mean charismatically taking over and commandeering the conversation. Instead, it means listening to what others are saying and appropriately responding and asking thoughtful questions.

This book provides you with 200 different conversation starters and questions that can help you build your confidence in speaking with others and be seen as a skilled conversationalist. As you have seen, these topics of conversation were separated into different social situations to help teach you the different conversational requirements.

However, there is more to being a good conversationalist than just asking the right questions. You must also listen to what your partners are saying and be aware of the conversational and social expectations of the situation.

In fact, to be a good conversationalist, you must talk as much as you listen. It is not always about talking the most, which is something that is lost on most people.

Hopefully, these tips will help you become the conversationalist you've always wanted to be. With a little practice, you'll find yourself more comfortable in conversations in no time.

REFERENCES

Griffin, J. (2018, November 26). *Six ways to be a great conversationalist.* Forbes.com. https://www.forbes.com/sites/jillgriffin/2018/11/26/six-ways-to-be-a-great-conversationalist/?sh=44a02d947f01

www.ingramcontent.com/pod-product-compliance
Lightning Source LLC
Chambersburg PA
CBHW050048260726
48658CB00005B/1837